Poet Tom Sexton invites us into a Volkswagen bus with four bald tires, and then drives us across the world. We don't look away from factory plumes, truck stops, and tour busses in Denali; this is a landscape of heart valves and "boneyard tailpipes." But riding along with us is ancient poet Li Bai, who helps us ward off the braggarts and trappers, and who helps us find "a sea of small pink flowers beginning / to open." The humble and visionary poet Tom Sexton shows us both how to look for heaven on this earth, and also how to begin to leave it. You won't want this ride to ever end.

—EMILY WALL associate professor of English at the University of Alaska Southeast, and author of *Liveaboard*

These poems cover long distances with a clear eye for the natural world and the magical gift to console. Under Sexton's masterful lyricism, humor and pathos join, making this collection a joy to read.

—JOHN MORGAN author of *Archives of the Air* and *River of Light: A Conversation with Kabir*

Form and content. Tom Sexton gives us on page after page small tight houses of language that provide shelter from chaos and places to savor what is good in life, each one a "momentary stay against confusion" as Robert Frost envisioned poems. We are grateful for his wide-ranging eye and keen ear, always attuned to the large and small animals, humans in their situations, and the landscape that we read forever.

—PAUL MARION author of *Union River: Poems and Sketches*

Li Bai Rides a
Celestial Dolphin Home

Tom Sexton

Text © 2018 University of Alaska Press

Published by
University of Alaska Press
P.O. Box 756240
Fairbanks, AK 99775-6240

Cover design by Martyn Schmoll.
Interior design by Publishers' Design and Production Services, Inc.

Cover image: Dolphin from iStock.

Right corner chop is the Chinese interpretation of "Tom Sexton." Designed by Fang Cun Stamp Carving.

Library of Congress Cataloging in Publication Data

Names: Sexton, Tom, 1940– author.
Title: Li Bai rides a celestial dolphin home / Tom Sexton.
Description: Fairbanks, AK : University of Alaska Press, [2018] |
Identifiers: LCCN 2017060275 (print) | LCCN 2018003388 (ebook) | ISBN 9781602233652 (ebook) | ISBN 9781602233645 (softcover : acid-free paper)
Classification: LCC PS3569.E88635 (ebook) | LCC PS3569.E88635 A6 2018 (print)| DDC 811/.54dc23
LC record available at https://lccn.loc.gov/2017060275

For Sharyn

Contents

An earlier version of "Homestead" appeared in *Cirque*.

Driving North

Snowy Egret Rising

On the night Li Bai tried to embrace the moon
in its fullness on the surface of the Yangtze River,
blossoms scented the air, and beyond the moon
pale stars powdered the sky. That faint shiver
of white near the surface was a dolphin rising.
I carry a book of his poems whenever I travel,
poems that touch the heart like a gentle snow.
Look, over there in that marsh, a snowy egret rising.

By the St. Croix River

Do you remember that October
afternoon when we were walking

by the St. Croix River, pausing
at pool after empty pool, you

wondering how it must have been
when river herring, countless

as the stars, were in every pool
and shallow, how we walked on

in silence until, like ancient
travelers on the Silk Road, we

came upon a tree, heavy with yellow
apples, how I'd been going on

about Yeats's silver apples of the moon,
his golden apples of the sun,

how you reached up and plucked one
that we devoured to its core,

how we walked on, almost holding
hands, almost young lovers again,

wet behind the ears, about to drive
north, glancing at our wedding bands.

Wachusett Reservoir

A blacksnake road
broken cloud
quarter moon shining

into the reservoir
like a torch held
by a ghost searching

for something left
behind when
the water began to rise

erasing four towns
from the Commonwealth
of Massachusetts

sound of a snipe
two more towns to go tonight.

Maids in Yellow

The radio promised a warm spring
day with forsythia beginning to open.
We were looking down from our room
at a group of hotel maids in yellow
waiting to dash across the street.
Taxis sent wave after wave across
the sidewalk to the stoop where they'd
taken shelter. The rain was biblical.

I imagined them floating across the street,
butterflies in a soft spring breeze
before landing on the other side, maids
once again, a bit of magical thinking
to comfort us, like a chocolate wrapped
in gold foil placed by a maid on your pillow.

Lake Utopia

A warm spring breeze from the lake
is moving the curtains in the bedroom
of a couple watching the light-kissed
mainsail of a sloop from their bed.
Classical then jazz fills the room.
They lift small cups of wild-civet coffee
to their lips. "A hint of citrus," he says.
"This must be paradise," she sighs.

A local barista arrives a little after dawn
every Sunday morning with their weekly order.
They leave her tip and the key in the mailbox.
If they see her pedaling along, they wave.
When it's raining, her bike's tires sound
just like Buddy Rich's brushes on their gravel.

West of Rousses Point, New York

In one of those otherwise forgettable small towns
a place where other people happen to be born,
a place where there are no sidewalks to roll up,
a place that proclaims it was the birthplace of
a minor leaguer who almost made it to the majors,
a man holding a small American flag is sitting in
an Adirondack chair and waving to passing cars,
even to the men wearing orange jumpsuits,
men looking out of a van with bars on its windows,
even to the woman in her beamer checking her cell.

Glen Nevis, Ontario

From a window in a former abbey, now an inn,
I watched mourners, mostly white-haired women
and a few old men, led by a piper playing
"Amazing Grace," as they left the Catholic church.
Worn down by age and toil, their backs curving
like the letter C in surname after surname
on the gravestones I read the day before,
taking note that my clan, McLeod, is there.

Slowly, taking fierce step after fierce step,
they moved as one toward the waiting grave,
a dark-skinned priest walking slowly behind.
"The young move away," the innkeeper said.
While shovels filled the grave, the piper played
again, softly now, like gently falling rain.

Superior Pulp, LLC

An acrid plume of steam shaped like a child's
bonnet rose into the early-morning sky

over the last mill in a town by a tannin-colored river.
Its main street a punch-drunk fighter

with most of his teeth knocked out.
Here a Lexus costs more than a house.

The pawn shop's sign reads "jewelry and guns."
No one was out for a morning run.

At 9:00 a.m. only the bowling alley's bar was open.
I needed a boilermaker and, perhaps, a smoke.

"That mill's the smell of money," the bartender said,
"if the Chinese owners shut her down, we're dead.

I look for that plume every single day.
When tourists like you stop by, we hold a parade."

Near Wawa, Ontario

On a trail through a stand of hemlock,
roots rising from thin soil like sea serpents
making their way to Lake Superior,
a trail I hoped led to a clearing where
years ago an Ojibway elder filled my hands
with blueberries from his coffee can,
I was looking for kindling to start a fire.
We devoured his gift in our leaking tent.

I tell myself the '60s are long gone. Thoreau
and Longfellow gather dust on a shelf.
That eagle overhead is probably a drone,
but when I reach a clearing that seems familiar,
I find a sea of small pink flowers beginning
to open. "I have more than enough," he said.

Elderly Couple Having Breakfast at a Truck Stop

She asks the waitress for water and begins to divide
the pills I watched her take from her purse.
Six are lined up before her, even more before him.
I recognize one: a low dose of rat poison to keep his heart
in rhythm. He pushes the one-a-day vitamin away
and breaks off a piece from the unbuttered toast
she ordered from the senior's menu to go with their tea.
She opens two packets of artificial sweetener
and begins to pour while he watches a truck driver
at another table waving a piece of bacon like a baton
at the trucker with him who's pouring maple syrup
on his pancakes. He chews his toast. When she notices them,
she says to him in a loud voice, "They'll be dead in a year,"
but he's already on the road, windows down, moving away.

In Praise of Surgeons

When he finished telling my wife
that her heart might be out of her
body for a while, if necessary, while
they replaced her valve, the same wife
reading a book as I write, he glanced
at me and asked if I had any questions.
Imagining her cold beneath a sheet,
I mumbled, "Where do you get your valves?"
He smiled slightly then said, "We don't
get them from Smithfield Packing. Your
wife's valve came from a pig that was
raised to save her life or someone else's.
If you don't have any other questions,
I'll see you both early tomorrow morning,"
as if we were going out for bacon and eggs.

Crossing the Prairies

Driving west, we came this way fifty years ago
when we were young and invincible,
singing Johnny Horton's "North to Alaska"
as we drove deep into the star-crowded night
in a Volkswagen bus with four bald tires
and a spare with its sidewall cracked,
back on the road at dawn running on caffeine.
Now we both bear fresh scars from a surgeon's
knife. Your heart no longer inviolate.
A long scar like a scimitar on my neck.
I watch your face when a voice on the radio
says, "My fields are beyond green with only
the slightest rot from rain, I'll harvest in a week."
On both sides of the road, the land is as flat
as a griddle. You could watch your dog run away
for a month as the old saw goes. We drink it in:
slight wind moving ripe grain, the endless sky,
wires sagging between poles, a red-tailed hawk.
"Beyond green," you say, "beyond green," then smile.

Yellow-Headed Blackbirds at Dusk

At dusk, on the puffy tip of every cattail
in a small Saskatchewan marsh,
bird after bird glows like the gold
on a newlywed's finger. The cattails
barely moved beneath their weight.
We'd been sniping at each other all day,
small things, over time love's narrowing.
How beautiful they were, those small birds
whose song's a rusty gate. Our hearts swung open.

The Man Behind the Wheel, Fort Nelson, B.C.

A man about my age drives past the once fashionable
Fort Nelson Hotel three times while I drink
a cup of bad coffee by the restaurant's front window.
Fewer and fewer people stay here on their way
to Alaska now that the road's been fully paved.
His Pontiac Parisienne, its suede roof peeling,
must have been his dream car when he was a teen,
when his '50s flattop looked cool not foolish.

On every pass, he slows down to look at the hotel
as if he's hoping to see the girl he didn't marry
or his younger self coming through the door.
"His mother raised him in a converted chicken coop,"
a woman sitting near me says to no one in particular.
I ask for a refill, wave when he drives by once again.

Alaska Highway Lodge, 1966

Four days north of Dawson Creek on a road
that was always dusty or slippery as a greased pig,
we paid eight dollars Canadian for two omelets
made with powdered eggs and powered milk
with homemade toast, white or brown,
a feast we devoured while we waited to see
if the lodge's mechanic could weld the hinge
on our VW's door that wouldn't stay closed.

The waitress said, "There's nothing he can't do,
nothing once he picks up his welder's torch."
Outside his shop, a boneyard of tailpipes
and radiators that looked like the shields
of a defeated army. Sparks flew around his head.
Was there really a pet wolf chained out back?

House Sparrows at Glennallen, Alaska

Like passengers who fell asleep
on a cross-country bus and woke
from a dream of a warm welcome
only to find themselves in a cold
and snowy landscape, they huddle
together, puffed up, shivering
on a small patch of snowless ground
beneath the heat vent of the only
store that's open in a town
half a continent from their home.
They're the buff color of those
old scuffed leather suitcases
that people once kept in closets
for their long dreamed of vacation.
A few chirps, then silence once again.

Under Heaven's River

A few years back when I was artist-in-residence at Denali National Park and Preserve, I spent almost two weeks at the cabin where the famous naturalist Adolph Murie lived while he studied the Tolkat River wolves who had a den not far from the cabin. I arrived early in June with my manual typewriter and enough food for my stay. I was looking forward to the solitude even though I knew the North Fork cabin was just off the road, a road that runs the length of the park. I wasn't expecting wilderness, but I was expecting solitude.

The morning after I arrived, busses started going by, busses that travel the park road all summer. I could see faces pressed to every window. The road is usually closed to private vehicles. I also wasn't prepared for the arrival of guests from a "wilderness" lodge at the end of the road who had a catered lunch not far from the cabin several times while I was there. Their bus is allowed to use the road.

In the cabin, I was surrounded by books of other Alaskan writers, including the work of two Fairbanks poets, John Morgan and Peggy Shumaker, who had been in residence before me, and I had the poems of both Li Bai and Wang Wei with me for company, two poets I return to again and again, poets who touched the very heart of nature before it was tamed. After all, I was there to write, solitude or not.

After several days of throwing away drafts, I decided to have Li Bai wake up at dawn in Broad Pass just outside the park after a night of heavy drinking to begin a summer of wandering. My goal was to find a way to send him home. The following eight-line poems, the line length used in the Chinese lu-shih, a form used by Li Bai, were begun during my stay.

I didn't see any wolves or bears on my long walks while I was staying at the cabin; however, on my last night there I was invited to read at one of the lodges close to the end of the road at Kantishna, a former mining camp. The road over Polychrome Pass, just beyond the cabin when you're headed west, is narrow, steep, and winding. I managed a white-knuckle drive over the pass one morning. I have acrophobia, so I was reluctant to try it again. It was decided that someone else, a young woman who was a park intern, would do the driving that night. Night in Alaska in June is a long twilight. I didn't complain. She was very good company, and I didn't have to look at the edge of the road where it dropped off. Something you have to do when you're driving.

On our ride back to the cabin around midnight, we met a brown bear the size of a Hummer. It was ambling down the road in front of us, moving about five miles per hour, and we were moving about two. Every once in a while, it would stop, look at us, and then continue on. It appeared to be smiling. After twenty minutes or so, it decided it had enough of us so it left the road and watched us go by. It still visits me in my dreams.

The following poems are my attempt to bring Li Bai home. My thanks to the staff at Denali National Park for making my stay possible.

Li Bai Wakes in Broad Pass

He woke beside a swift glacial stream below
mountains rising from still brown foothills,
foothills as drab as a worn boot. His head hurt.
How much wine had he drunk the night before?
Where were his new friends who said his poems
dimmed the moon and made the dawn blush?
They called him a Banished Immortal, so he'd be
fine even though his tongue had turned to sand.

Li Bai and the Magpie

"How is your family?" Li Bai asked the magpie
who had been following him since he woke.
"Fine and thank you for asking," the magpie replied,
then he flew off and returned with western clothing
to replace Li Bai's torn gown. "You'll blend in wearing
these, and my wife will quickly mend your gown
with feathers she's been saving for just such a task.
Walk toward the tallest mountain and you'll be safe."

Magpie's Wife

She mended Li Bai's gown with feathers and a little
fur from a snowshoe hare then hid it in an old nest
of grass and sticks they had abandoned years ago.
Magpie decided to follow Li Bai's progress from one
river valley to another to keep his new friend company.
"He has a beautiful voice, he could almost be one
of us if he could fly, and he doesn't need lightning
to start a fire," he told his wife. "I really like his style."

Li Bai Meets a Brown Bear

When Li Bai saw the bear ahead of him on the tundra,
he was speechless, dumbstruck, and he'd seen bears
when he wandered Jade Dragon Snow Mountain.
When the bear turned its massive head to look at him,
Li Bai quickly composed a poem in its honor,
a poem about the bear's generous nature and courage.
When the bear paused to listen, Li Bai also paused,
then he rolled his shoulders side to side like the bear.

The Brown Bear

He decided to follow Li Bai while he wandered
from valley to valley, fishing in every stream,
catching a few grayling, and digging up roots.
Perhaps he felt a kinship with another old man.
He felt sad when he heard Li Bai chanting.
One night, he left a lake trout by his campfire.
Not even a poet could survive on grayling.
But the chattering magpie who was always at Li Bai's
side got on his nerves so he left, but he didn't go far.

Trapper

Would he ever find a familiar stream, one that would
take him home even if this was a dream, Li Bai wondered.
Walking a gravel bar, he looked up to see a man
wearing the head of a wolf for a hat coming his way.
"I'm a recreational trapper," the man said to Li Bai.
"I set my traps just outside the park every winter."
Li Bai didn't say a word so the trapper continued on.
Attached to its own head, the wolf's tail moved as if it were alive.

Li Bai Arrives at Wonder Lake

He looked at the great snow-covered mountain beyond the lake
for a long time before something in the shallows caught his eye.
"I've stood on Denali's summit in both summer and winter,"
the man beside him bragged. He was certain that Li Bai
was just another Chinese tourist who had come to see Denali,
one who had wandered away from his group to get a better look.
"You should honor it with your absence, a mountain as great
as the one before us needs its privacy," Li Bai whispered in his ear.

Almost Fall

When Li Bai left Wonder Lake, he was deep in thought.
He had arrived in spring and now it was almost fall.
His old bones ached and he missed his friends.
Below new snow on the mountains, the tundra
was just beginning to turn red, reminding him
of the hint of rouge on a beautiful courtesan's cheek.
When the moon rose, he cast a long shadow.
Even magpie felt his sadness and for once was silent.

The North Fork Wolves

Li Bai reached the North Fork of the Tolkat River
just as the wolves, three young males and a female,
appeared at the mouth of their den and began to sing
their pleasure at the full moon's rising, their pleasure
at being alive. Li Bai listened and when the wolves
fell silent for a moment, he answered their song
with his own, both songs rising and falling as one.
The wolves have all been killed as I write these lines.

Li Bai Discovers Adolph Murie's Cabin

How have I missed this small cabin close to the road,
he thought? Once inside, he found my stack of books
and those left by writers who had been there before me.
He also discovered my wine. Someone must be studying
for his civil service exam hoping to attract the Emperor's eye,
he must have thought when he saw my copy of the *Analects*.
When he finished the wine, he left a note on my typewriter
that read: Study the poems of Li Bai and find a better wine.

Coal Creek

I was carrying a dog-eared copy of his poems
to read while I sat on a ridge above the North Fork
of the Tolkat River where I was told I might see a wolf
from the mythic pack that Adolph Murie studied.
While I watched for wolves, Li Bai drank my wine.
Night was still a shadow, but I knew that before long
the Milky Way, his Heaven's River, would be visible.
No wolves appeared, but I now knew how to send him home.

Heaven's River

Li Bai put on his mended gown when he reached
the summit of Polychrome Pass. It was dark
for the first time since he arrived. Heaven's River
was flowing overhead. He lifted his arms and his gown
became a sail that carried him out of sight,
a sail made possible by Mrs. Magpie's skillful sewing.
Tourists watching from the season's last bus
must have thought he was a comet or a shooting star.

Li Bai Rides a Celestial Dolphin Home

He wasn't worried as he rose toward Heaven's River
where a celestial dolphin was waiting to be his guide,
a dolphin who took pity on him because he'd seen
Li Bai chanting to dolphins in the Yangtze River.
When the Three Gorges appeared, Li Bai dismounted
and plunged to earth. Some farmers working in their fields
just before dawn thought they saw a shooting star.
Others said it was only the poet Li Bai coming home.

The Brown Bear's Lament

He was eating blueberries when he looked up
and saw something rising from Polychrome Pass,
a golden eagle perhaps because a pair nested nearby,
but he soon realized that it was the tall man
whose pantomime made him roll over laughing.
He stood on his hind legs swaying from side to side,
his large teeth clicking, his voice a low moan,
a lament for a friend he would never see again.

The Magpies Build a Nest in Honor of Li Bai

Sorrow filled their days after Li Bai departed
while Mrs. Magpie was attending to a family crisis
brought on by a fledgling. To ease their grief,
they built a nest of twigs and the silken thread
she had saved when she mended Li Bai's gown,
a nest they placed high in his favorite cottonwood
so on the shortest day it would hold the rising
moon's first light. "Like an egg," Mrs. Magpie sighed.

Coda:

The last of the North Fork wolves have been killed by trappers
according to those who studied them, and Li Bai's dolphins,
baiji, have vanished from the Yangtze River never to return.
The Three Gorges have been dammed, but we can still imagine
that Magpies can talk when they want to, that celestial dolphins
swim in Heaven's River even though all our instruments tell us
that's impossible. We must imagine a world made whole again
and live in a way that helps make it possible.

Let us hope that somewhere wolves will always sing, and brown
bears eat their fill of berries, that the wild if not wilderness will never
disappear, that it is possible to believe a shooting star can portent
the birth of a Banished Immortal as one did according to legend
on the night Li Bai was conceived.

Two Photographs

Russian American Bells

Did they once speak to the faithful
from the belfry of a wooden church,
their blue domes wet with mist,
these bells in a nineteenth-century album?
I cannot read the Slavonic script
around the bottom of each bell,
if it's Slavonic and not a design
intended for the eye of God alone.
In place of a cherub, the figure
of a shaman rides the smallest bell,
a trill, so he can keep an eye on
the goings on below and those above.

Russian Orthodox Priest

Pribilov Islands, circa 1880

Asiatic features composed, he looks down
from the altar at the photographer's lens.
The villagers are on the rookery clubbing
seals. One earthly czar has replaced another.
Behind him, an otherworldly light seems
about to flood the church. Is that halo
around his head part of the iconostasis?
Then, as they have before, my eyes settle
on three fingers visible above the crosses
on his chasuble, so vulnerable, so human.

The Night Sky

Richardson Homestead

In Memory of John and Jo Haines

1.

From the window of the cabin he built
using the wide planks of an old bridge,

they watched the light narrow, day
after day, until another long winter arrived

and hunger sat between them at the table,
like an uninvited guest who refuses to leave,

until their nerves rattled like chains
and the last fat disappeared from the pot.

He waited for good news to arrive in the mail.
She painted birds on small pieces of bark.

Wearing her bright red hat, the one I saw
in a photograph, she was the first to leave.

He could be as cold as ice, indifferent.
A couple from Fairbanks bought the place.

2.

The last time I stopped, what remained of the cover
of their old greenhouse was flapping in the wind

like the sail of a Viking longship arrived to carry
their lingering spirits over Banner Dome,

over the blood-red tundra they knew so well,
over the ghosts of the ancient Dorset people,

over the vanishing polar ice and into the star-
timbered shaft we know as myth where Odin

waits with a raven sitting on each shoulder
while the poet Bragi plucks a harp made of stone.

Black-Capped Chickadee

A black-capped chickadee rises from October's tall grass
its feathers gray as the cold fog beginning to lift after three days.
From the ridge where I'm walking, I can see the homeless camp below.

Paper Birch

Oldest of all the trees in our yard,
it was a spindly sapling on that snowy
day when we moved in many years ago.
Now it's a candelabra for the stars
when winter nights are long and deep.
When the days begin to lengthen, leaves
appear overnight, or so it always seems.
October's gold drifts down while we sleep.

Christmas Wolves

Close enough to the city that we could hear
traffic, three wolves, motionless, like stone,
watched as we entered a small clearing.
The largest, the color of frost, was flanked
by the others so they could easily close
on us or vanish into the woods. They didn't
move as they watched us hurry away. "Don't
tell anyone," my wife whispered, "not a soul."

Rime Ice

If angels exist, even the imaginary kind,
I imagine they'd come down on a night

such as this when everything's covered
with rime: those glowing lanterns

I saw hanging from a mountain ash,
the antenna on my neighbor's roof.

They'd hold their great wings wide,
feathered with light, lighter than rime.

Making Applesauce on a Snowy Afternoon

Who was first to bring the scent of simmering
apples sprinkled with cinnamon and sugar
together? Could it have been Adam and Eve
in their cold hut outside the Gates of Eden?
Was it the serpent trying to make amends?
Let the snow fall and the cold wind blow
until all the kitchen windows disappear.
My applesauce is simmering on the stove.

Common Merganser on a Winter Morning

The merganser, with the iridescent-green head
and orange beak that reminded me of the orange

I hoped to find at the bottom of my Christmas stocking
when I was a boy should have migrated to open water

when the lagoon began to freeze. Yesterday it was still
diving in a small iris of swiftly moving water.

Would I have felt this way when I was young?
Its underbody was as white as new snow.

Snow Squall

At dusk, a feint, a swirl of flakes, before
the wind quickened and the squall arrived,

a great white bear slipping one paw through
a slightly open window, while its other paw

tried the door before retreating with a hiss.
When the wind eased, we opened the door.

It was now a boat being rowed to the west.
Stars swam in its wake like small silver fish.

Snow-Blind Rivers

To the north, it's already dark,
the moon rising pale
as a moth's wing

over the Tanana Valley, over
Denali's blue shadow,

over the snow-blind rivers: Chena,
Nenana, Tanana.
How sad it

must be to not love the moon,
its river of flowing light.

Benediction

For Dave and Eli

In the generous light of a full moon
falling on a pond, a family

is skating in a line, father to youngest
daughter, the mother in the middle.

The days are beginning to lengthen,
but for now, the ice is still firm.

Their runners flare as they turn
toward a barrel glowing on the shore

where a few pussy willows lift
their small white cups, fill them with light.

Goldfinches at a Feeder

For Joy McCall

A cold winter and a colder spring will lead
to nothing good, I was mumbling to myself
when suddenly they appeared at our feeder
just after dawn with deep snow on the ground,
their bright yellow feathers the only hint of color.
Their wings were a sooty black as if they'd
almost flown too close to the sun like poor Icarus
and had just returned to make my poor heart sing.

Saw-Whet Owl in a Hemlock Tree

It's dusk. I look up to see a saw-whet owl
looking down, a monk wearing a cowl.
It's late November. Winter's moving in my bones.
Was it hunting for voles when I came along?
It's small enough to have fallen from God's pocket
when he was busy arranging the stars and planets.
Would you like to be in a poem, I almost say?
It tilts its head. Perhaps it's listening to the stars.

A Magical Fox

Our Christmas glogg was warming
on the woodstove when we left our cabin

for a neighbor's across the marsh
when winter's first aurora appeared.

I almost dropped his present, two jars
of cloudberry jam thick with yellow berries.

Finnish folklore claims a magical fox
creates it by moving his tail, I said,

and he's busy tonight. If it touches
the mountains, he wants us to dance;

and, dance we did, looking up for clues,
powdery snow rising with our every step

until the sound of a semi downshifting
on a nearby hill, its lights touching

the tallest spruce for a moment
broke the spell and our dancing ended.

When we crossed the marsh on the way
back to our cabin long after midnight

stars poured like milk across the sky.
And that was enough, more than enough.

The Winter Sky

Long ago according to the book I'm reading
there was once a rabbi who read the Torah
from dawn to dusk, decade after decade
trying to understand the meaning of his life.
One night, too restless to sleep, he looked up
at the winter sky and saw a shooting star,
a scroll that opened and closed in a blink.
A morsel for a mouse, he thought, but enough.

A handful of stars had appeared when I closed
the book on my desk. Another long winter
was coming to its end. I thought of swans
moving their great wings, shadowing the prairies
below. I thought of birch in the boreal forest
unfurling their small leaves, waiting for rain.

Moonlight

According to those who know, the moon's light
is a mere reflection, and the moon a stepping-

stone, a chip-shot from the earth,
but as I look up at it tonight high above

the snow-dusted mountains to the east,
I'm a satellite, a lover, an acolyte.

Beside me, my faithful companion, old age,
both of us looking up, our eyes wide, besotted.

In Praise of Visible Things

For Brent and Linda

The red-necked grebes that suddenly
appeared on the lagoon on the day
the ice disappeared have left their nest
of roots, roots pulled from the bottom
of a shallow cove. I watched them build
it root by root using twigs for mortar.
Wild calla lilies are now blooming in the nest,
opening their trumpet-like yellow blossoms.

Away from the nest, a new chick is riding
on its mother's back. The male is watching.
And far to the west, a faint wash of light
is fading slowly from the evening sky.
Tomorrow will bring another angle, another
slant of light, another watcher, watching.

Basho

Before he was Basho, he called himself Green Peach
to honor the Chinese poet Li Bai, called White Plum
by his admirers. Late spring snow on our apple tree.

Thinking of Basho While Walking at Dawn

For Mike McCormick

When he was an old man
with hair as white as Fuji's,
Basho still longed to wander

the countryside and not sit
with students in his haiku hut.
Hearts blossom on the road.

My hair is white. When I leave
my house, I can see Denali,
a mere toddler in mountain years.

Greening

Where all winter there was frozen clay and ice,
today there is grass that seems to have grown
tall overnight, the way they say hope can grow
in the heart, can lighten your step. Suddenly
a triad of sandhill cranes rises from the flats
making the morning sky quiver with their calls.
They're here early I think as I watch them
disappear toward mountains still covered with snow.

In This the First Long Light of Spring

For Emily Wall

Thin from their long winter fast,
three white birch and one aspen
on a south facing slope
where the snow is melting fast,
drinking their fill, nodding
to each other as if they're
old friends catching up on the news,
wondering who'll be first to swell
in this the first long light of spring.

At Delta Junction

A few days before the summer solstice
near the eastern edge of a field
bright with new grass at almost midnight,
a young bull moose with velvet covering
its antlers the way a glove covers a hand.
It turns its head to watch my every step.
Far beyond the field, new snow on the Alaska
Range rising into a sky that's wide and endless.
A convoy of cumulus is moving north.
At my feet, strawberries almost ripe.

Tom Sexton is the founder of the creative writing program at the University of Alaska, Anchorage, as well as a former poet laureate of Alaska. His books include *For the Sake of Light* and *A Ladder of Cranes*, both from the University of Alaska Press.